THE YOUNG PERSON'S GUIDE TO MONEY

Zach De Gregorio

Wolves & Finance

This book contains information on personal finance and investing. Laws affecting personal finance decisions vary from state to state. It is recommended to contact a professional advisor before making financial decisions. Neither the publisher nor author shall be liable for any loss of profit or any other commercial damages, including but not limited to special, incidental, consequential, or other damages.

ISBN-13: 978-0692898130

WOLVES AND FINANCE INC.
Las Cruces, NM
www.WolvesAndFinance.com
For inquiries contact zach@WolvesAndFinance.com
Printed in the United States of America

This book is dedicated to Fabian Bahe.

You taught me how to value the truly important things in life.

TABLE OF CONTENTS

INTRODUCTION

In High School, I bounced my first check. I remember feeling upset, scared, ashamed and uncertain how it even happened. In a conversation with my Grandmother, I shared my frustration over my money mistake. She told me a powerful idea. She said, "If you can figure out the money part of life, your life gets so much better."

I have found this idea to be true. So many people struggle with money. Money causes pain and creates roadblocks for their lives. It does not have to be this way. Money can be a source of joy in your life. Money can enable you to achieve your dreams.

I write this book to give young people valuable tips on money.

Like me, many young people are unprepared for the money problems they will face as they start out in life. Speaking from my own experience, my teachers in school did not teach me about money, and my parents did not teach me about money. If someone does not teach you about money, you must learn those lessons the hard way.

I know I am not the only person with this experience, so I want to share with you some key lessons about money. If someone had given me this book when I was younger, I could have avoided so much unnecessary pain and hardship. Money plays a major role in your life. If you can learn these lessons early, you will be happier and have more money.

I meant this book to be short, straight to the point, and deliver tremendous value. Chapter 1 covers three big ideas about money. The remaining chapters each focus on a different area of your finances. I wish you the best of luck on your financial journey!

BIG IDEAS ON MONEY

I want to share with you three big ideas on money. These ideas are not intuitive, and many people do not follow them. However, if you embrace these three simple ideas, it can have a powerful effect on your finances.

Big Idea 1: Money problems are simple.

If you break down any money problem, I have found the solution is always simple. Most people think the opposite. People think money problems are complicated. People struggle over money problems. But you do not need to let money problems overwhelm you. The answer is simple. It will involve either figuring out how to make more money, or cut costs. That is it! It is that simple.

Money problems can be scary. I am not making light of what is probably a difficult situation. The solution will probably require sacrifice and hard work. To make matters worse, it may take a long time to work your way out of your situation. However, I recommend changing your perspective. Do not become overwhelmed and overcomplicate the problem. Instead, focus on a simple plan to solve the problem and then implement that plan.

The bottom line: If you have money problems, do not be scared. Make a plan to overcome it.

Big Idea 2: The problem is not the money. The problem is you.

Do not waste your time blaming money. Or other people. Or evil corporations. Or politicians. These are common complaints for money problems. When people find themselves in difficult situations, their first instinct is to blame someone else. But your financial situation is a direct result of the choices you make. If you are in a money problem, YOU made a bad decision, and may still be making bad decisions.

As soon as you realize that you are the reason for your money problems, you can start to fix them. You are in control of your situation. If you start making better financial decisions, your finances will improve.

The reason people do not take responsibility for their problems, is because the solution often requires significant sacrifices in their lives. Here are a few examples of solutions to money problems:

- Get a second job
- Stop eating out at restaurants
- Move to a cheaper home
- Drink tap water instead of buying drinks from the store
- Shop at discount clothing stores

- Spend your free time training for a better job

These examples are not attractive things that people want to do. But, if you are honest with yourself, you have the power to improve your financial situation. Make the sacrifice necessary to reach your money goals.

The bottom line: Take ownership of your problems.

Big Idea 3: Savings beats all other financial decisions

You can solve all money problems through saving money. Many studies show that a person's savings activities is the primary reason they accumulate wealth. It is more important than investing decisions. It is more important than what job you take. This is such a valuable lesson to understand: *Saving money is important.*

Let me explain what "saving" looks like. Every time you receive a paycheck from your job, you should not spend all of it. You should only be spending a portion of your check to live on. The rest of your check is savings. Either this money stays in your bank, or you can use it for investing, or paying off debt. This little bit of money you save every payday will grow and grow and grow. This savings helps you deal with any money problem that comes along in your life.

Many people do not save anything. They live paycheck to paycheck. When someone puts money in their hands, they instantly spend all of it. This is dangerous, because if something unexpected happens in your life, like your car breaks down, you do not have any money to deal with it.

The reason saving money is so difficult is that it requires self-discipline. Saving money is hard. When someone puts money in your hands, you have to not spend all of it, but instead put some of it aside for the future. This is what we call "delayed gratification." If you can learn to have self-discipline, savings will lead you to financial freedom.

The bottom line: Save money out of every paycheck.

MONEY EDUCATION

One of the biggest lessons about money you can learn… is that you should always be learning. Making good money choices requires continual education throughout your life. Different phases of your life require you to make different choices about money. For instance, you will make different decisions when you are first starting your career, than when you are entering retirement.

There are many different areas of finances to learn and explore. The remaining chapters in this book will cover many of them at a very high level. I will not be providing many specifics, because depending on your situation, you can research different areas on your own in more depth.

The goal of this book is to provide you with the overall understanding of the different money situations you will face when you are just starting out on your own. It is my hope that this knowledge will help you avoid some major money mistakes, and set you on the path to a positive financial journey.

The bottom line: Always be learning about money.

BUDGET

udgeting is the first money skill everyone needs to master. I cannot tell you how many young people I have heard say the words, "I just cannot manage to stick to a budget. Oh well." This attitude will hold you back from so many amazing things in life. If you can manage your money with a smart budget, life becomes so much better.

It is simple to create a budget. There are two steps:

1) Know your monthly expenses.

2) Make sure your monthly income is greater than your expenses.

That is it! It sounds easy, but you have to put in a lot of work and self-discipline to use a budget. There are many different budgeting methods out there. Use any of them. Just pick one of them and use it.

The central idea with a budget is not to spend more money than you bring in. This has two benefits. First, you will never have to worry about running out of money in your bank account. Second, you will have savings every month that will grow over time. You can stretch this idea and save as much of your income as possible every month. If you have a large amount of savings every month, you can accumulate a lot of money very quickly.

Many people underestimate the positive mental impact of having a sound budget. Knowing that you have your expenses covered every month provides you with great peace of mind. When people do not have a budget, they do not know if they are spending more than their income. Their spending is out of control, and this creates a lot of fear and confusion. You want to avoid this. Putting in the effort to use a budget, gives you control over your money, and avoids many money problems.

Once you consistently follow a budget, an annual budget review can help you get even more benefits. Every year you can review your budget and ask yourself two questions.

1) How can I cut costs?
2) How can I make more money?

This process takes a lot of thought, but can be a powerful way to make your financial choices more effective.

The bottom line: Create a budget. Follow your budget. Review your budget once a year.

SAVING

The more you can save, the better your financial life will be. I mentioned savings before in the chapter on the "Big Ideas on Money." Savings is so important that it also gets its own chapter. You determine your savings by your monthly budget. You want to save a portion of your income each month. You can save 10%, 20%, or even 50% of your income each month. Saving is a choice. The more you can save, the better off you will be.

So what do you do with all this money (Isn't that a great question to be able to ask)? You generally spend savings in three ways.

1) Get out of debt
2) Have an emergency fund

3) Build money towards your goals (house, travel, retirement, etc.)

You want to tackle debt first. I recommend avoiding debt, especially when you are younger. However, if you have accumulated debt (student loans, credit cards, car loans) focus on getting out of debt as soon as possible. Debt payments come out of your income every month. If you get rid of the debt, you can use all that money towards your other financial goals. What makes things worse is that debt charges you interest which is needlessly costing you money. You should not have any credit card debt. So use your savings every month to pay down your debt until it is all gone.

Once your debt is gone, you can start building up an emergency fund. An emergency fund is just a large amount of money that you can access whenever you need. The amount of money is really up to you, but a general rule of thumb is six months of living expenses. The reason an emergency fund is so amazing is it gives you incredible peace of mind. Your car may break down and you will not have to worry whether you have the money to fix it. You might have a sudden medical issue, and you will have the money to deal with it. Life throws you many curve balls, and this emergency fund will help you be prepared.

Once you are debt free, and have an emergency fund, then the FUN begins. You can build up savings towards any of your goals. This is going to depend on what you want out of life. You decide. You decide what kind of retirement you want. You can save for a house. You can save for a trip. You can start a business. You can invest. Once you have savings, you can start making choices with your money. Compare that to someone's life who has no savings. If you are living paycheck to paycheck, you have very limited choices.

Savings is hard. It means you are going to get money, and decide not to spend it. Instead, you will put it aside to spend on a later day. That takes discipline. This is especially hard when you are young, and you are not making very much money. But you need to learn the skill of saving as early as possible. Once you start to see your savings account grow, it becomes fun. You realize you are taking control of your life, and it becomes easier to save even more money.

The bottom line: Develop the self-discipline to save every month. Nothing will improve your finances as much as savings.

RENT

Rent is generally your greatest monthly expense. Most young people rent an apartment when they first start out on their own. You need to realize a few things about rent, because it has such a large impact on your budget.

First, if you have never paid rent before, you need to understand how expensive it is. Rent costs a lot of money. Rent varies a lot depending on the city you live in. I recommend going online and getting an idea of how much apartments cost in your area. For an example, let us just say your apartment costs $1,000 per month. That is $12,000 per year. If you were to make $24,000 in income each year, rent would take half of your money. You also have to realize, there are other costs as well. The cost for electricity and internet are also major expenses. It is important to realize how much rent is going to cost you.

Second, you need to realize how important it is that someone never evicts you from an apartment. If you miss paying your rent, your property owner can kick you out of the apartment. People refer to this as an eviction. Eviction laws are different in each state, but generally, if you do not pay your rent, property owners can evict you. An eviction will show up on your credit report. Apartment managers check your credit report every time you rent a new apartment. So if you ever get an eviction, it becomes very difficult to find a place to live. If you have a proper savings plan, you should never have to worry about missing a rent payment. But if money is ever tight for some reason, you should always prioritize paying your rent over other bills. It is easier to live without a working phone, than it is without a roof over your head.

The bottom line: Be prepared to pay rent, and always pay on time.

GETTING A JOB

The greatest impact on your budget is your salary. If you have been working on your budget, you realize this very quickly. If you make more money, you can spend more money. Your salary is like a ceiling, and the higher you can raise the ceiling, the easier your finances become. So getting a job is important.

You should treat your job with respect, because it is so important. You should treat your boss with respect, because they are your source of income. Your boss is not your friend. I am often surprised at how flippantly young people treat their job by showing up late, dressing sloppy, and generally acting unprofessional. Work is a great opportunity to earn money. If you perform well at work, you may even get the chance to earn more money through a promotion.

Avoid unemployment at all costs. If you are thinking of leaving your job, do not leave until you have another one lined up. You need to keep your income. If you find yourself suddenly unemployed, find another job as quickly as possible. Work anywhere you can add value. It does not have to be your dream job. The longer you stay unemployed, the less attractive you are to prospective employers.

While you are working, it is also helpful to look for opportunities outside your job that can supplement your income. This could be starting a business on the side. It could be selling your old furniture online. Any way you can generate money, will add to your monthly budget. These additional income streams will also help if you lose your job. If a side business does well, you could even make that your full time job.

You should always aggressively pursue increasing your income. Go after promotions. Keep your eyes open for better job opportunities. Get additional training and education to make your skills more valuable. You are building a career, and it is up to you to figure out ways to create value that will result in more income.

The bottom line: Your source of income is important. Treat it wisely.

BANKS

It will help your finances if you educate yourself on how banks work. I realize that banks can be intimidating. But banks are a necessary part of life. Banks are the institutions that everyone uses to hold their money. If banks did not exist, everyone would have to keep all their money in a safe in their homes. It is so much easier to have everyone keep their money in banks, and transfer money to each other by swiping debit cards. Checks are getting used less frequently as debit cards become more popular. Realize that debit cards are different than credit cards. Debit cards take cash right out of your bank account, whereas credit cards allow you to make charges that you have to pay off later (see the chapter on Credit Cards). So whether you are keeping your money in a bank, or you are doing business with someone else's bank, you will likely become a frequent customer of banks.

The first thing you will need from a bank is a checking account. A checking account will allow you to write checks and use a debit card. This is easier than carrying cash around all the time, and both methods transfer the cash directly from your account to make a purchase. It is important to note that when you write a check, there is often a delay. So it is important to keep track of your account balance. You should always know how much money is in your account before you make a transaction. An overdraft occurs, if you write a check for a higher amount than is in your account. If this happens, your bank can charge you high fees, and the company you are doing business with can also charge you fees. So you want to avoid this. It is easy to avoid this problem if you always know how much is in your account. This is easy today, because it is quite simple to check your account balance on your phone or computer.

You also need to be aware that people are always trying to steal your account information. So it is important to treat your account information carefully. If someone steals your account information, they can take your money right out of your bank. This type of identity theft is becoming more common. This is another reason to check your account balance frequently for any transactions you did not make. If this happens, contact your bank immediately and they will work with you to correct the error and get your money back.

It is helpful to realize that there are many different types of banks. There are big banks, smaller regional banks, and credit unions. Each type of bank has different strengths and weaknesses. For instance, big banks can offer many different services that the smaller banks may not be able to offer. On the other hand, smaller banks can offer more personal attention and customer service that is difficult for bigger banks. You do not want to move your account to different banks very often, because you want to be able to show a stable banking history. But it is also okay to have accounts with different banks, and shop around to see what institutions work best for you.

The main role of a bank is to lend money. This may not be important to you when you are just starting out. Most young people are not asking for loans. But it is useful to realize that you may need a loan down the road. So what you are doing when you set up a checking account at a bank, is you are setting the stage to ask for a loan ten years from now. Your transactions with your checking account is establishing a history with the bank. Let us imagine that in the future you want to buy a house. When you ask for a home loan, the bank is going to look at your history. They will decide whether to approve or deny giving you a large amount of money. The bank bases this decision on whether or not they trust that you will pay the money back over time with interest. So that is why it is important to not overdraft your checking account, and always deal with your bank accounts responsibly.

The bottom line: Get a checking account and check your balance often.

INVESTING

Investing in the stock market is risky. Do not put your money at risk unless you are willing to lose it all.

Start investing early. The reason for this is that investing takes a long time to learn. It takes someone decades of learning to make good investment decisions. Investing is complicated. Financial markets are complicated. So the earlier you can start learning about investing, and practice will small amounts of money, the better off you will be later in life. Even if you are never a big investor, understanding how the stock market reacts will help you in your career as you make strategic decisions at your company.

You do not have to use a lot of money. It is okay to start out by investing $50 or $100. What you are doing is learning. Some people might be nervous and want to learn before they put their money at risk. But I recommend the opposite. As long as it is a small amount, go ahead and make a small investment. Online investing platforms today are easy and cheap to use to purchase stock in companies. You learn a lot more when you have your own money at risk. Watch how the market reacts as your investment changes value over time. Watch how YOU react as your investment moves up and down. Getting the "feel" of the market takes time and experience. You not only have to learn about how the market works, you have to control your own emotions about market movements.

The first thing you have to learn about investing is diversification. This one tactic will save you from losing a lot of money. Diversification means it is better to buy multiple stocks instead of putting all your money in one stock. This is an example of the famous saying "Don't put all your eggs in one basket." If you buy smaller batches of multiple stocks, if one stock loses money, you still have money in the other stocks. This can be frustrating if you have one stock that does really well, while the rest are not as good. But you have to realize that over the long term, you will have a much stronger financial performance because you are protecting against the downside risk.

A common way to invest is 401k plans. Your company will likely have some form of investment plan like a 401k. It is good to realize that 401k plans can vary greatly between employers. Some plans can be better than others. You should research your specific company's plan and decide whether it makes sense for you.

The bottom line: Start investing early with small amounts and always diversify.

Investing in the stock market is risky. Do not put your money at risk unless you are willing to lose it all.

INSURANCE

Insurance is another complicated area like investing that you want to start learning about early. Paying for insurance can be tough when you are starting out when you may not have the funds in your budget. However, a small investment in insurance each month can save you from some potentially big financial disasters.

The main concept of insurance is that you never want to have to use your insurance. You are paying a bill every month for something you hope, you never use. I realize this is difficult to understand. Even if insurance protects you, you do not want bad things to happen. Unfortunately, in life, bad things do happen. Insurance helps you get through those events. So it is helpful to plan your insurance coverage before tragedy happens.

Car insurance is the first form of insurance you will likely need. The law requires you to get at least minimum coverage. In the event you get in a car accident, your insurance will help cover the damage that occurs. If you are just starting out, and have a cheap car, it might not make sense to get more insurance coverage than this. You make this decision by comparing the monthly payments of the additional insurance with the value the insurance company will pay you to replace your car if you damage it beyond repair. Check the Kelley Blue Book value of your car to see if the monthly payment is worth it.

This is a great example of how insurance works. You value your potential loss in the event of a tragedy, and determine how much insurance to purchase that would get you through the event. If you have a very expensive car, then it makes a lot of sense to purchase more insurance to provide you greater protection in the event of a loss.

Another form of insurance you will need is health insurance. Your first job will likely provide health coverage through your employer. Everyone's health insurance options are different, so you have to evaluate your own situation. My personal opinion, if I have the option, is to select higher levels of health insurance, even though I am a healthy individual. The problem with lower levels of insurance is you generally have more difficulty dealing with the insurance company. You might have a smaller selection of doctors to choose from, and you have to argue more with the insurance company about what treatments are covered and how much money they will pay. Since health insurance is primarily for major unexpected health accidents that occur, you do not want to be arguing with the insurance company about your coverage when you really need it.

Renter's insurance is another form of insurance that is useful if you are just starting out and renting an apartment. This insurance is usually relatively inexpensive and a good investment. What would happen if your neighbor starts a fire and burns down the apartment building? It is not your fault, but you would still find all of your belongings ruined. You would come home one day to find you have lost everything, and have nowhere to live. Do you have the money to replace all your clothes, furniture, computer, and pay for a hotel? Buying renter's insurance protects you in this type of situation.

The bottom line: Look into purchasing car insurance, health insurance, and renter's insurance.

CREDIT CARDS

You need to realize that credit cards are DANGEROUS. Most financial advisors tell people never to use credit cards. The reason why they do this is they are so tired of seeing people ruin their lives with credit cards, that they just tell everyone to stop using them. I tend not to take such an extreme position. Credit cards do have benefits and are convenient, especially when you are traveling. I think credit cards have a place, as long as you realize they are dangerous. Before you get a credit card, you must realize that the majority of people in life NEVER acquire the self-discipline necessary to use a credit card responsibly. As a result, they encounter bad money problems. Realize that credit card companies have departments of hundreds of people whose sole job is to get you to spend more money; often times money you do not have to spend.

The key to successfully using credit cards is self-discipline. The way a credit card works is a bank issues you "credit." This credit is a certain spending limit that you can use for purchases with the promise that you will pay it back at some point in the future. So the bank is giving you the ability to buy things, not with your money, but with the bank's money. Of course, you have to pay the bank back, and that is where people get into trouble. People will buy things, without having the money to pay their bills, and then the bank charges high interest on your debt and fees for missing payments.

The only way to avoid this problem is self-discipline. You need the self-discipline only to make purchases you have the money to pay back. Even though you have the ability to buy things with your credit, do not make those purchases unless you have the money.

What I recommend is to test yourself before getting a credit card to see if you have enough self-discipline with money. You can test yourself with your budget. Set an aggressive savings plan with your budget every month. This means you are going to set aside money not to spend. If you can successfully save this money every month FOR AN ENTIRE YEAR and not spend it, you likely have enough self-discipline for a credit card. If you find you do not have this self-discipline, do not get a credit card. Not everyone has to use one. You can get by with just using cash and your checking account.

If you do decide to get a credit card, here is my recommendations to avoid problems.

1. Never charge anything on your credit card you do not already have the cash to purchase.

2. Check your bank account before the purchase to confirm you have enough cash to pay the bill.

3. After you make the purchase, set aside the money to pay the bill in your bank account.
4. Pay the entire bill immediately when it comes at the end of the month.
5. Always pay your credit cards on time, just like any other bills. Late payments show up when banks calculate your FICO score, which is a sign of your credit.

The bottom line: Realize that credit cards are dangerous. If you get a credit card, pay off the entire bill every month.

STUDENT LOANS

Many young people sign up for student loans without knowing what they are doing. I am not going to argue about whether student loans are good or bad. My goal is to provide you with insight into what student loans mean for your life. Young people go to college, and sign the paperwork for massive loans without realizing the consequences of their actions.

A student loan is an agreement with a bank. If you are going to college, student loans will likely be part of your journey. A bank is providing you with money to pay for college, and you agree to pay the bank back over a long period of time with interest.

What many people do not realize, is the size of the monthly loan payments after graduation. If you borrow a large amount, the loan payments can be a huge portion of your paycheck each month. The consequences of not making student loan payments are pretty bad. This means you have to prioritize your life around paying back your large debts.

The impact this has on your life, is you will likely have to delay things you might want, so that you can prioritize getting a steady paycheck. Your monthly student loan bill will dictate your life choices. Getting a steady paycheck means, you will likely need to work for a large corporation, and then do whatever it takes to keep that job. You have agreed with the bank to do this for the next 20 years of your life. Some examples of what this means is:

- Delaying buying your own house
- Delaying starting a family
- Not having a nice car
- Not living in the city you want, but where your corporation tells you

- Not taking the job you want, but working in the position your corporation needs

The key idea people need to understand is that signing up for a student loan is a major life decision. You are making a tradeoff. The benefit of student loans is that college opens up many opportunities for rewarding professional careers. The negative aspect of student loans is you are prioritizing your career in a corporation over other opportunities in life. Your other option is not to go to college, but then you need to accept that you are giving up becoming a professional like a doctor, lawyer, or accountant. You will have to pursue a different career path.

Another recommendation is to look for ways to graduate college early. Graduating a year early can shave an enormous amount off your student loan debt.

The bottom line: Before you sign any student loan document, make sure you are comfortable with the major life decision you are making.

LEGAL ISSUES

This is not necessarily financial, but I included it in the book because it can greatly affect your finances. I find that young people generally understand they should not break the law. But many people do not fully realize how bad the consequences of criminal actions are. If you choose to do activities that are illegal, it can damage your life in ways where you might not be able to recover. Laws vary in different states and countries, so take some time to research your local laws.

Drugs. Do not take illegal substances. The laws around drug use vary, but some of the consequences are really bad, including jail time. Additionally, drug charges will show up on your record. Every time you apply for a job, the company will run a background check. Your conviction will show up and your past drug use will be taken into consideration when you are compared against other job applicants. This of course seriously limits the types of jobs where people will be willing to hire you.

Felony. Do not commit a felony. This includes serious crimes like stealing, aggravated assault, tax evasion, fraud, etc. Just like drug convictions, felonies will show up on background checks when you apply for jobs.

DUI. Do not drink and drive. If you go out to a bar to drink, please take a taxi home. The cost of the taxi is worth it! There are serious consequences to driving drunk, including the danger to yourself and others. If you get a DUI, you have court costs and greatly increased car insurance rates. Sometimes the cost of insurance will increase so much, you will no longer be able to afford to own a car. DUI's also show up in background checks when you apply for jobs. Pay to get a taxi. Do not chance getting a DUI. Imagine the horrible situation, if you drove drunk, hit someone else and killed them. Please avoid this situation by taking a taxi home.

Sex offender laws. Sex crimes are horrible and so society rightfully gives significant consequences for these crimes. You do not want to be registered as a sex offender. This usually is the result of a conviction of rape, indecent exposure, or other sexual crime. It would be wise never to put yourself in a situation where someone could accuse you of inappropriate activity. If you become a sex offender, your name, photo, and contact information is published online. Depending on the state, you may be required to remain on the sex offender registry for the rest of your life.

As a general rule of thumb, life is much better if you just follow the rules.

There are so many great things to explore in life; you should not waste any of your time doing something illegal.

The bottom line: Do not be a criminal.

BUYING A HOUSE

Many young people are eager to purchase their own home. There are many good reasons for home ownership. Some of the benefits include tax benefits, freedom to renovate, joining a good neighborhood, and achieving a dream. The two biggest mistakes I see people make when purchasing a house are:

1. **Buying a house too soon.** There is no rush to buy a house when you are young. It is okay to rent for a while. This gives you the opportunity to save your money and focus on achieving good finances before you buy a house.

2. **Buying more house then you can afford.** Many people purchase a home at the top of their price range. This means they have to stretch their finances to make the mortgage

payment each month. It is much more manageable to purchase a home you can easily afford, so you have extra money to make repairs and upgrades as needed.

The key to buying a home is to wait. This is a major purchase that you will spend a long time paying off. Take your time. You do not even want to start looking for a home until you are confident with your finances. This way your home purchase can be a source of joy, rather than cause you stress.

The bottom line: Rent while you are young. Buy a home later.

BUYING A CAR

T his one simple trick to buying a car will save you a lot of money and headaches: *Buy your cars with cash.* Car dealerships today offer you many different options to finance a new or used car. Do not use fancy financing. Do not get a car loan. Do not get a lease. Only buy a car with cash.

The reason for this rule is that cars lose their value so quickly. Let's think about this. The average life expectancy of a car is around 8 years. If you purchase a car for $10,000 that means it drops in value by $1,250 each year! So if you tried to sell it after one year, someone would likely only pay you $8,750 for the car. You need to realize how quickly your car drops in value. If you were to take out a loan to buy a new car, within one year the car would likely be worth less money than the debt you owe. That means if you sold the car, the money from the sale would not be enough to pay off the loan. You would still be paying loan payments on a car you no longer own!

It is tough not to fall for the dealership's sales pitch. Everyone wants a shiny new car. The downside to not using financing to purchase a car is you will not be able to afford something as nice. However, the benefit is you will own the car outright. You will not have to make monthly car payments, and instead you can put that monthly expense into savings.

The bottom line: Buy your car outright with cash.

CREDIT REPORT

All young people should realize they have a financial report card called the "credit report." This report captures all your financial activities. Your activities stay on this report for seven to ten years. Items on this report include credit cards, car loans, student loans, home loans, rental activity, late payments, and loan defaults. The credit report companies also use this report to generate your FICO score, which is a number that represents how attractive your credit report looks.

Businesses can check this report and your FICO score to get an idea of your "credit worthiness." Any time you do business with a company, ask for a loan from a bank, sign up for a cell phone, rent an apartment, or apply for a job, people can check your credit report. This is your financial reputation written down. People read this report to find out how good you are with money.

Bad items will show up on this report. If you have paid your credit card late, it will show up as a negative mark, and a bank might reject you for a loan or require you to pay a higher interest rate. You can check your own credit report online once a year. It is free. It is a good idea to work to correct any negative marks on your report. The ideal situation is to have a flawless credit report, so anyone checking will see you are good with your money.

The bottom line: Check your credit report once a year and work to correct any flaws.

FINAL THOUGHTS

I hope I was able to provide some insight and helpful tips and tricks about money.

This is just the beginning of your financial journey. Always be learning about money.

Let me leave you with this thought. It is possible to remove the pain from people's lives caused by money problems. There is so much hardship and sadness around money. It does not have to be this way. It just takes learning about how money works.

Money should be a source of joy in your life and not a frustration. Once you master money, your life gets so much better.

"THE BOTTOM LINE" FROM EACH SECTION

1. If you have money problems, do not be scared. Make a plan to overcome it.
2. Take ownership of your problems.
3. Save money out of every paycheck.
4. Always be learning about money.
5. Create a budget. Follow your budget. Review your budget once a year.
6. Develop the self-discipline to save every month. Nothing will improve your finances as much as savings.
7. Be prepared to pay rent, and always pay on time.
8. Your source of income is important. Treat it wisely.
9. Get a checking account and check your balance often.

10. Start investing early with small amounts and always diversify.
11. Look into purchasing car insurance, health insurance, and renter's insurance.
12. Realize that credit cards are dangerous. If you get a credit card, pay off the entire bill every month.
13. Before you sign any student loan document, make sure you are comfortable with the major life decision you are making.
14. Do not be a criminal.
15. Rent while you are young. Buy a home later.
16. Buy your car outright with cash.
17. Check your credit report once a year and work to correct any flaws.

To get more information, check out the website www.WolvesAndFinance.com

To email Zach De Gregorio with feedback on this book, send an email to zach@WolvesAndFinance.com

About the Author:

Zach De Gregorio, CPA is the current CFO (Chief Financial Officer) at Spaceport America. Drawing on his experience in multiple sectors including high-tech, aerospace, energy, entertainment, telecommunications, real estate, and hospitality, Zach empowers organizations to use their money effectively.

Zach De Gregorio has a Bachelor Degree from the University of Southern California in Los Angeles. He also holds a M.B.A in Finance from Arizona State University and a Master of Accounting Degree from the University of New Mexico.

Zach lives in Las Cruces, NM and enjoys trail-running in the beautiful New Mexico landscape.